How to
UKULELE

CONTENTS

GORDON PRICE MUSIC LTD.
10828 Whyte Avenue
EDMONTON, ALBERTA T6E 2B3
(403) 439-0007

THE
UKULELE

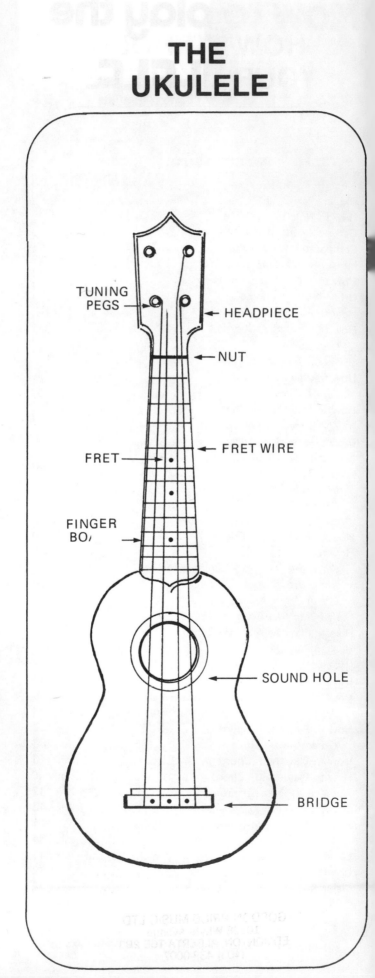

TUNING PEGS → HEADPIECE

→ NUT

→ FRET WIRE

FRET →

FINGER BO/ →

→ SOUND HOLE

→ BRIDGE

HOW TO HOLD YOUR UKULELE

When playing, keep your left wrist away from the fingerboard. This will allow your fingers to be in a better position to finger the chords. Press your fingers firmly, but make certain they do not touch the neighboring strings. You may strum with the backs of the fingers of the right hand or use a felt pick. The pick is held between the thumb and index finger.

Getting Acquainted With Music

Musical sounds are indicated by symbols called NOTES. Their time value is determined by their color (white or black) and by stems and flags attached to the note:

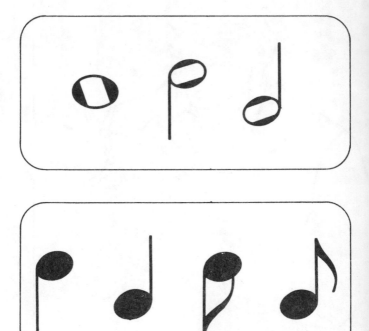

The notes are named after the first seven letters of the alphabet (A-G), endlessly repeated to embrace the entire range of musical sound. The name and pitch of the note is determined by its position on five horizontal lines, and the spaces between, called the . . .

STAFF

————— 5th LINE - F —————
                                          4th SPACE - E
————— 4th LINE - D —————
                                          3rd SPACE - C
————— 3rd LINE - B —————
                                          2nd SPACE - A
————— 2nd LINE - G —————
                                          1st SPACE - F
————— 1st LINE - E —————

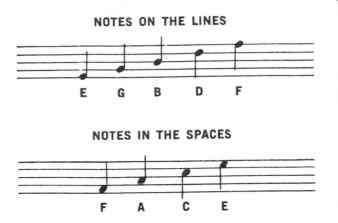

NOTES ON THE LINES

E G B D F

NOTES IN THE SPACES

F A C E

Music is also divided into equal parts, called . . .

MEASURES

One measure is divided from another by a BAR LINE

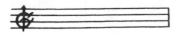

During the evolution of musical notation, the staff had from 2 to 20 lines, and symbols were invented to locate certain lines and the pitch of the note on that line. These symbols were called . . .

CLEFS

Music has three clefs, the C, F and G clefs. The entire range of the Mandolin can be written in the G clef. Originally the Gothic letter G was used on a four-line staff to establish the pitch of G:

It grew into the modern

Comparative Note Values

The WHOLE NOTE

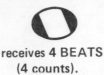

receives 4 BEATS
(4 counts).

The DOTTED HALF NOTE

receives 3 BEATS.

The HALF NOTE

receives 2 BEATS.

The DOTTED QUARTER NOTE

receives 1½ BEATS.

The QUARTER NOTE

receives 1 BEAT.

The EIGHTH NOTE

receives 1/2 BEAT.

Measures

Music is divided into equal parts
called MEASURES. A BAR LINE
divides one measure from another.

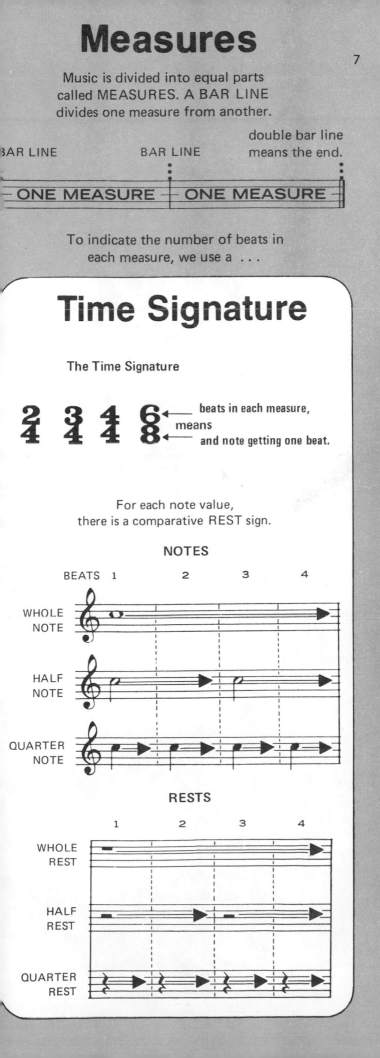

BAR LINE   BAR LINE

double bar line
means the end.

— ONE MEASURE — ONE MEASURE —

To indicate the number of beats in
each measure, we use a . . .

Time Signature

The Time Signature

$\frac{2}{4}$ $\frac{3}{4}$ $\frac{4}{4}$ $\frac{6}{8}$ ← beats in each measure,
means
← and note getting one beat.

For each note value,
there is a comparative REST sign.

NOTES

BEATS 1   2   3   4

WHOLE NOTE

HALF NOTE

QUARTER NOTE

RESTS

1   2   3   4

WHOLE REST

HALF REST

QUARTER REST

HOW TO TUNE YOUR UKULELE

The four strings of your ukulele are the same pitch as the four notes shown on the piano in the following illustration:

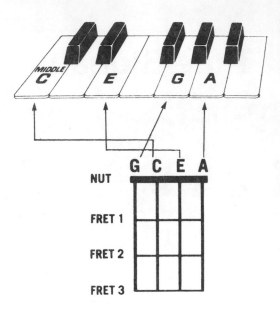

Pitch pipes are also useful for tuning and are available at your local music store or studio.

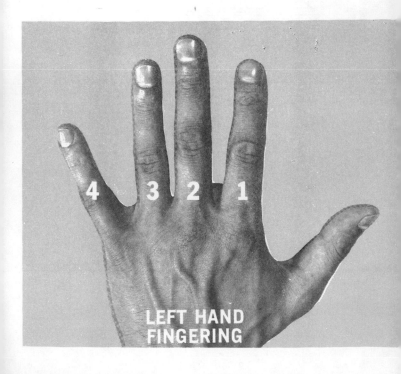

LEFT HAND FINGERING

OTHER WAYS OF TUNING YOUR UKULELE

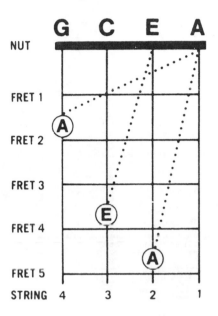

Tune the 1st string to A on the piano. If no piano is available, approximate A as best you can and proceed as follows:

- Press 5th fret of 2nd string to equal pitch of 1st string (A).
- Press 4th fret of 3rd string to equal pitch of 2nd string (F).
- Press 2nd fret of 4th string to equal pitch of 1st string (A).

CHORD CHART

If a string has an O over the string, it means it is an "open" string. It is strummed, but not fingered.

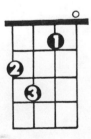

Numbers in circles represent finger numbers. Press down on the frets indicated with your left hand (see page 8) and strum the proper strings with your right.

HOW TO PLAY THE G7 CHORD

Place ❶ and ❷ in position, then play 1 string at a time:

Play 4 strings together

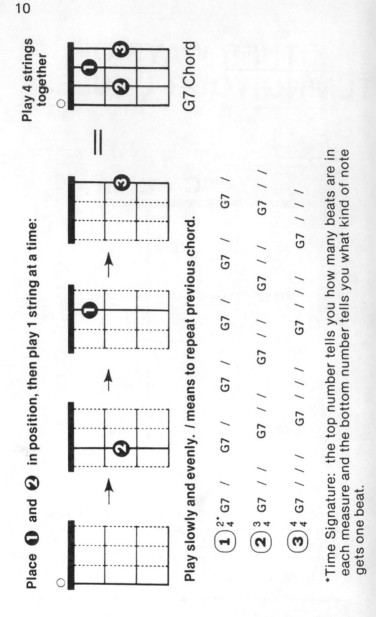

G7 Chord

Play slowly and evenly. / means to repeat previous chord.

(1) $\frac{2^*}{4}$ G7 / G7 / G7 / G7 / G7 / G7 /

(2) $\frac{3}{4}$ G7 // G7 // G7 // G7 // G7 //

(3) $\frac{4}{4}$ G7 /// G7 /// G7 /// G7 /// G7 ///

*Time Signature: the top number tells you how many beats are in each measure and the bottom number tells you what kind of note gets one beat.

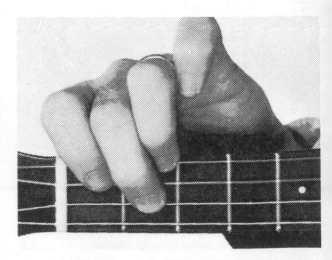

HOW TO PLAY THE C CHORD

Place ❶ and ❷ in position, then play 1 string at a time:

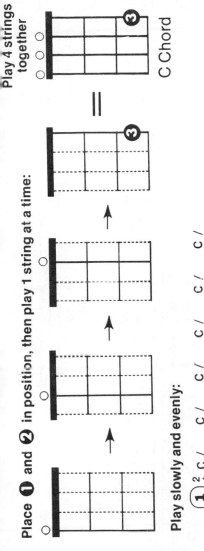

Play 4 strings together

= **C Chord**

Play slowly and evenly:

① $\frac{2}{4}$ C / C / C / C / C /

② $\frac{3}{4}$ C / / C / / C / / C / /

Repeat each line several times:

③ $\frac{4}{4}$ C / / / G7 / / / C / / / G7 / / /

④ $\frac{3}{4}$ C / / G7 / / C / / G7 / /

⑤ $\frac{2}{4}$ C / G7 / C / G7 / C G7 C 𝄽*

* 𝄽 means Rest (silence for 1 beat)

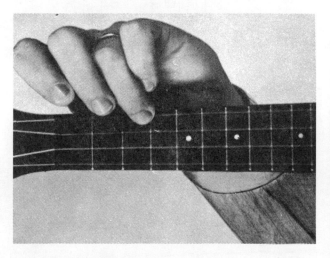

11

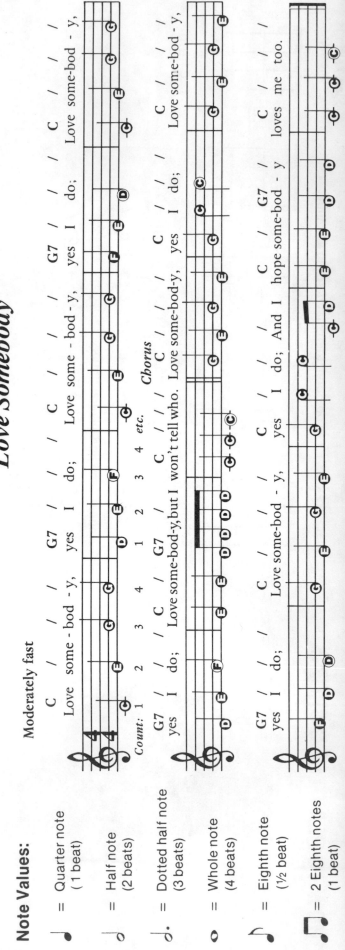

Love Somebody

Note Values:

♩	=	Quarter note (1 beat)
♩	=	Half note (2 beats)
♩.	=	Dotted half note (3 beats)
𝅝	=	Whole note (4 beats)
♪	=	Eighth note (½ beat)
♫	=	2 Eighth notes (1 beat)

12

Sweet Betsy From Pike

*This is an incomplete measure. The missing beat is in the 1st measure.
Many songs begin with an incomplete measure.

HOW TO PLAY THE G CHORD

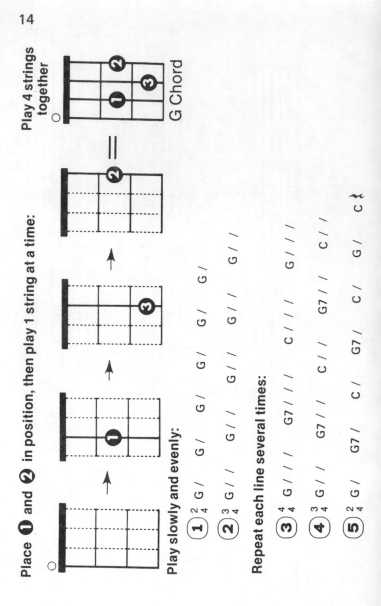

Place ❶ and ❷ in position, then play 1 string at a time:

Play 4 strings together

G Chord

Play slowly and evenly:

① $^2_4$ G / G / G / G / G /

② $^3_4$ G / / G / / G / / G / /

Repeat each line several times:

③ $^4_4$ G / / / G7 / / / C / / / G / / /

④ $^3_4$ G / / G7 / / C / / G7 / / C / /

⑤ $^2_4$ G / G7 / C / G7 / C / G / C ⸾

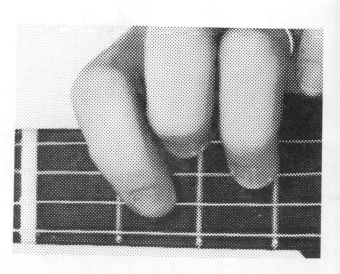

Tom Dooley

HOW TO PLAY THE D7 CHORD

Place ❶, ❷ and ❸ in position, then play 1 string at a time:

Play 4 strings together

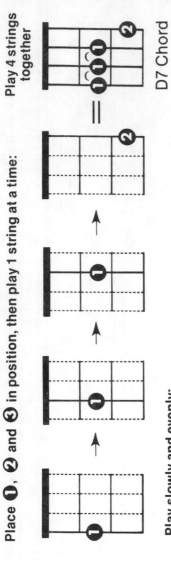

D7 Chord

Play slowly and evenly:

① $\frac{2}{4}$ D7 / D7 / D7 / D7 / D7 /

② $\frac{3}{4}$ D7 / / D7 / / D7 / / D7 / /

Repeat each line several times:

③ $\frac{4}{4}$ G / / / G7 / / / C / / / D7 / / / G

④ $\frac{3}{4}$ G / / C / / D7 / / C / / / G

⑤ $\frac{2}{4}$ G / G7 / C / D7 / G / C D7 G

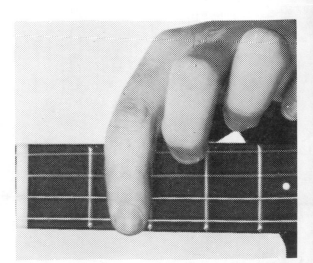

The Streets of Laredo

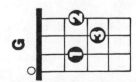

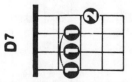

17

Cockles and Mussels

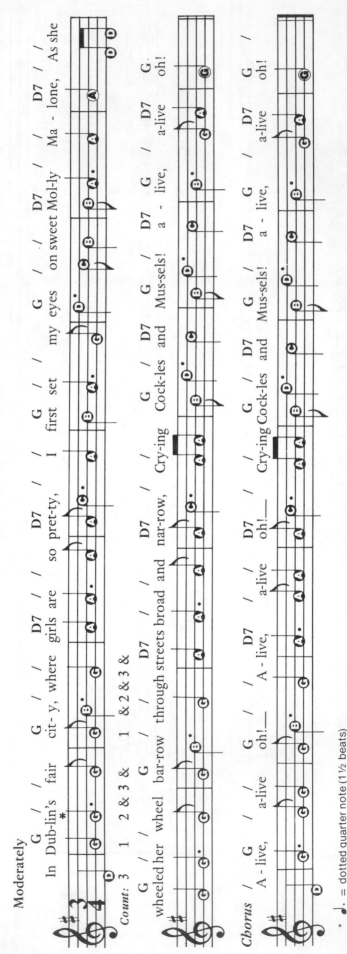

Foggy, Foggy Dew

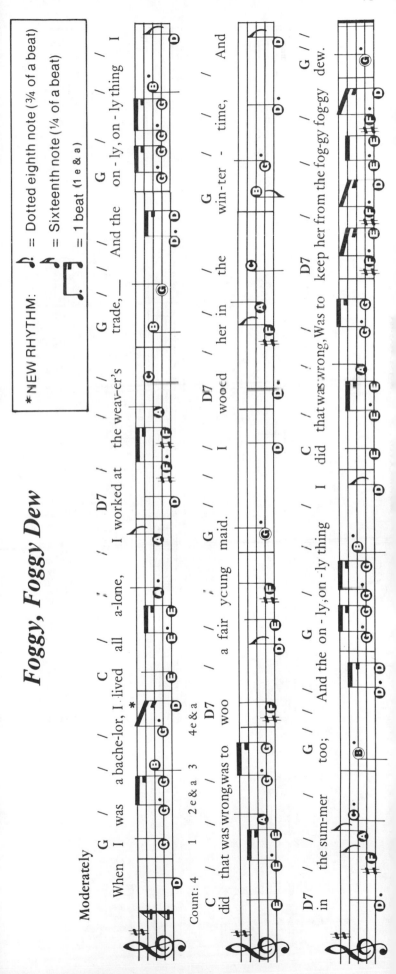

*NEW RHYTHM: ♪. = Dotted eighth note (¾ of a beat)
♪ = Sixteenth note (¼ of a beat)
= 1 beat (1 e & a)

Moderately

When I was a bache-lor, I lived all a-lone, I worked at the weav-er's trade, — And the on-ly, on-ly thing I

Count: 4 1 2 e & a 3 4 e & a

did that was wrong, was to woo a fair young maid. I wooed her in the win-ter - time, And

did that was wrong, Was to keep her from the fog-gy fog-gy dew.

in the sum-mer too; And the on-ly, on-ly thing I

Old Dan Tucker

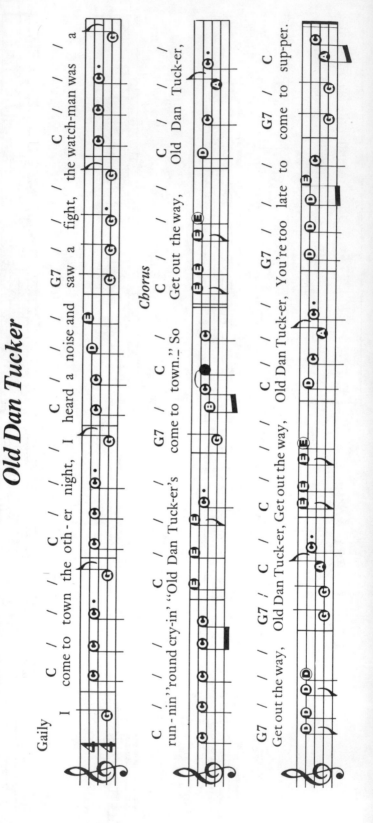

Gaily
I come to town the oth-er night, I heard a noise and saw a fight, the watch-man was a

run-nin' 'round cry-in' "Old Dan Tuck-er's come to town." So

Chorus
Get out the way, Old Dan Tuck-er,

Get out the way, Old Dan Tuck-er, Get out the way,

You're too late to come to sup-per.

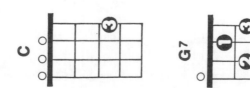

C

G7

Blue-Tail Fly

* This sign is called a FERMATA. It means HOLD the note or chord longer (about twice as long is usually enough).

𝄾 = Eighth rest (½ of a beat).

Careless Love

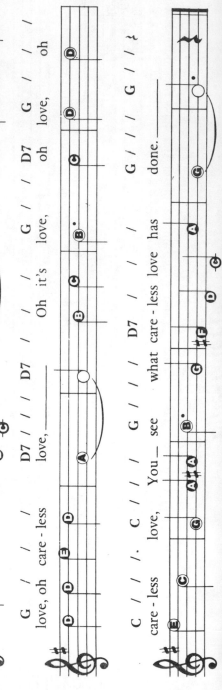
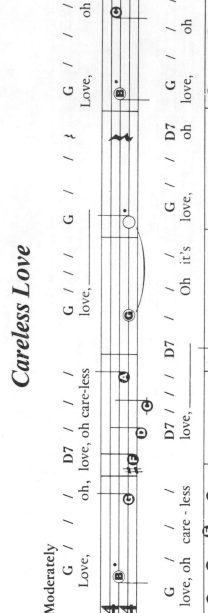
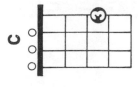
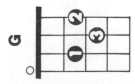

Michael, Row the Boat Ashore

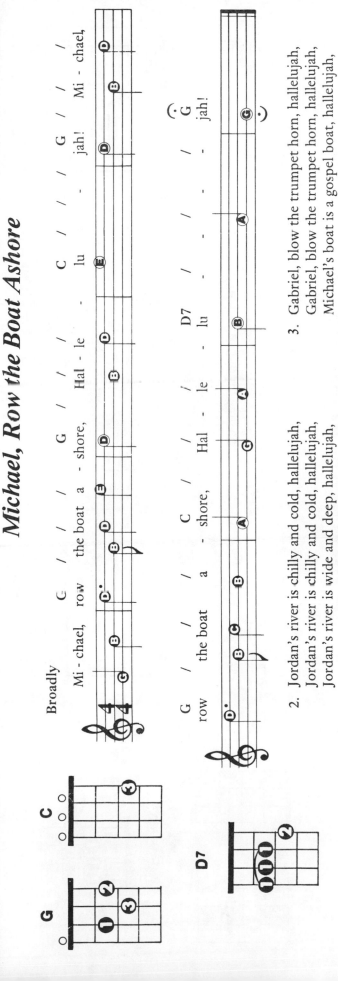

2. Jordan's river is chilly and cold, hallelujah,
   Jordan's river is chilly and cold, hallelujah,
   Jordan's river is wide and deep, hallelujah,
   Jordan's river is wide and deep, hallelujah.

3. Gabriel, blow the trumpet horn, hallelujah,
   Gabriel, blow the trumpet horn, hallelujah,
   Michael's boat is a gospel boat, hallelujah,
   Michael's boat is a gospel boat, hallelujah.

HOW TO PLAY THE A7 CHORD

To play this "bar" chord, the G and E strings should be pressed with the side of your 1st finger.

Place **❶**, **❷** and **❸** in position, then play 1 string at a time:

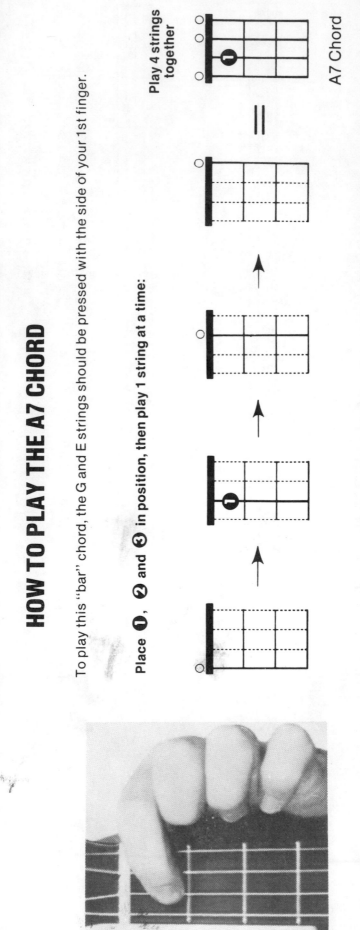

Play 4 strings together

A7 Chord

HOW TO PLAY THE D CHORD

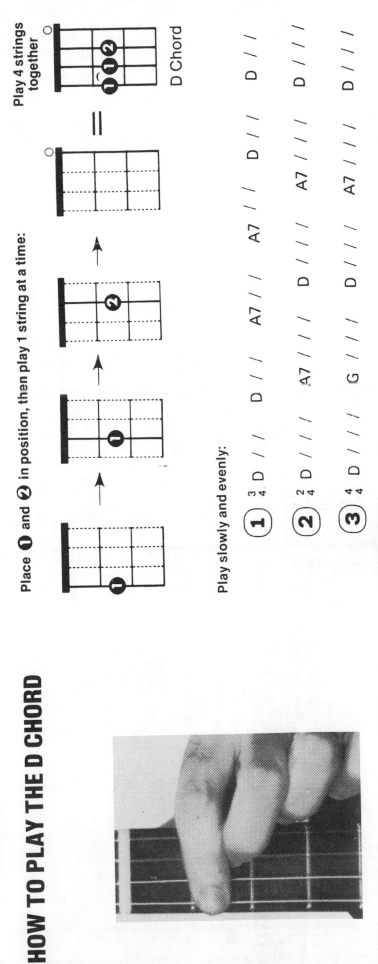

Place ❶ and ❷ in position, then play 1 string at a time:

Play 4 strings together

D Chord

Play slowly and evenly:

① ³/₄ D / / D / / A7 / / D / / A7 / / A7 / / D / /

② ²/₄ D / / / A7 / / / D / / / A7 / / / D / / /

③ ⁴/₄ D / / / G / / / D / / / A7 / / / D / / /

When the Saints Go Marching In

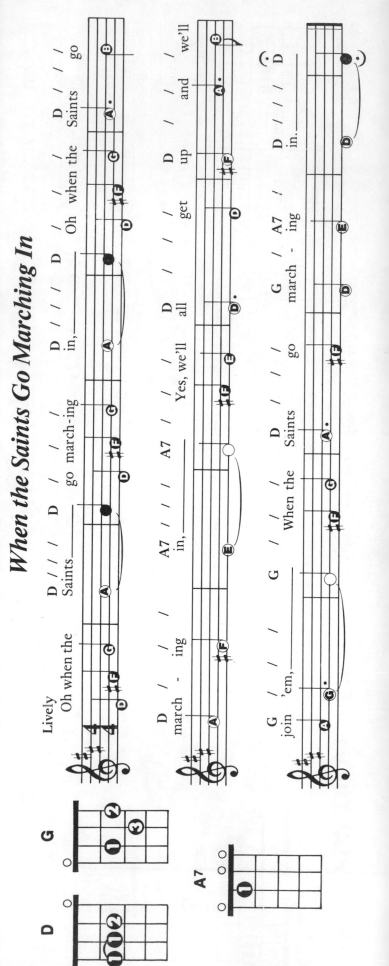

Little Brown Jug

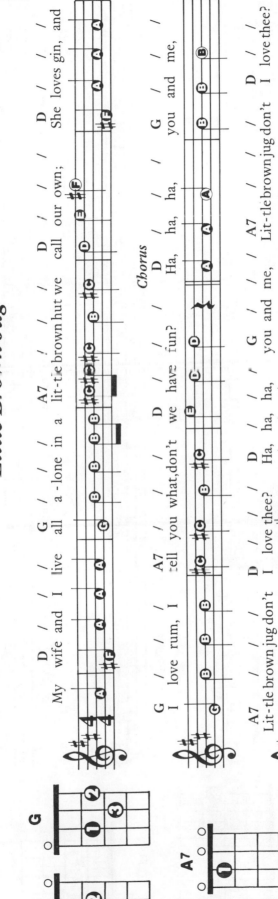

Green Grow the Lilacs

The Red River Valley

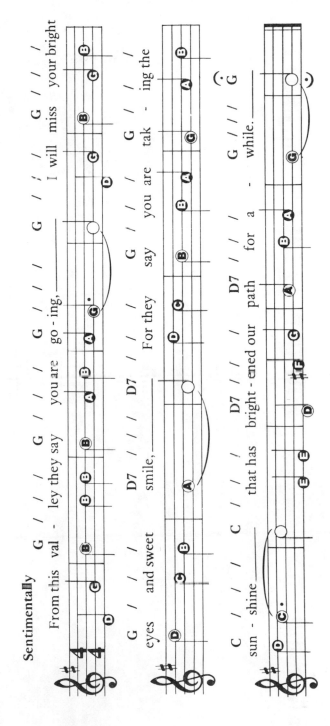

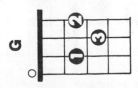

HOW TO PLAY THE E MINOR CHORD

So far we have been playing major and seventh chords. Another classification of chords is minor. They have a melancholy sound and are usually used to depict a sad and wistful mood.

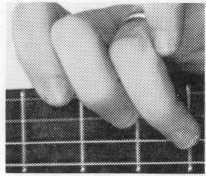

Em

HOW TO PLAY THE A CHORD

A

Up to this point we have been striking the strings with a down stroke of the pick. We may achieve a richer, more satisfying accompaniment style by using both down *and* up stroking.

Experiment with this type of strumming when playing the following songs. Also go back and try this technique with the songs you've already played.

⊓ = Down stroke of the right hand pick.

V = Up stroke of the right hand pick.

Play slowly and evenly:

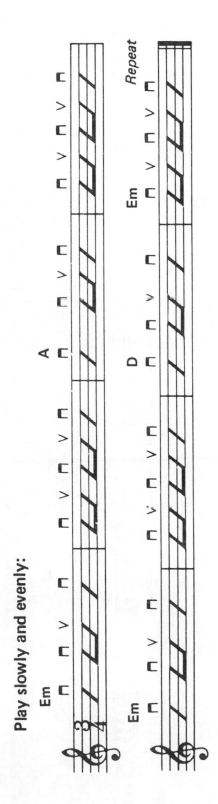

Scarborough Fair

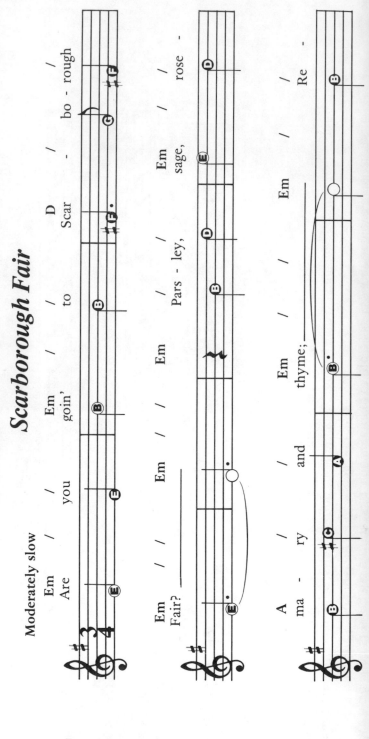

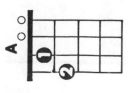

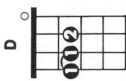

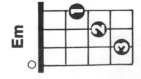

Scarborough Fair (cont.)

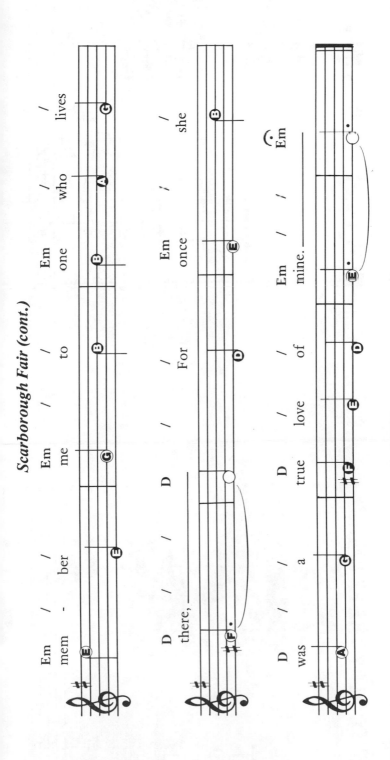

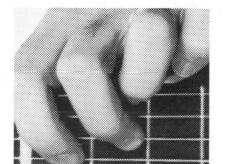

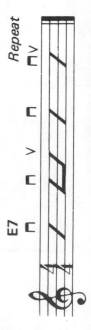

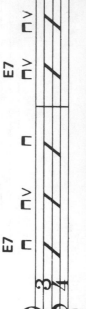

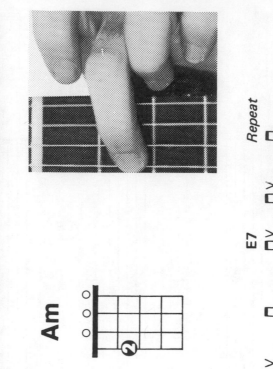

HOW TO PLAY THE A MINOR CHORD

Am

E7   E7   E7   *Repeat*

HOW TO PLAY THE E7 CHORD

E7

E7   *Repeat*

E7 AND A MINOR CHORDS
(cont.)

Play slowly and evenly:

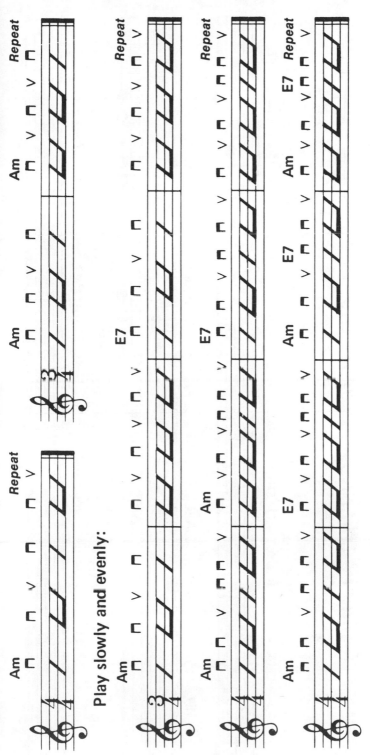

Joshua Fought the Battle of Jericho

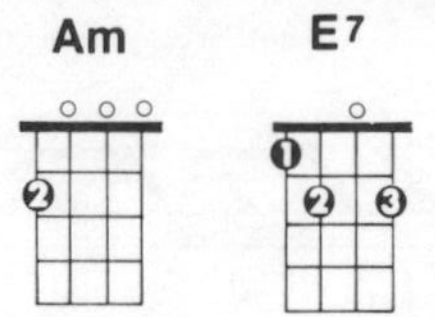

Moderately Fast

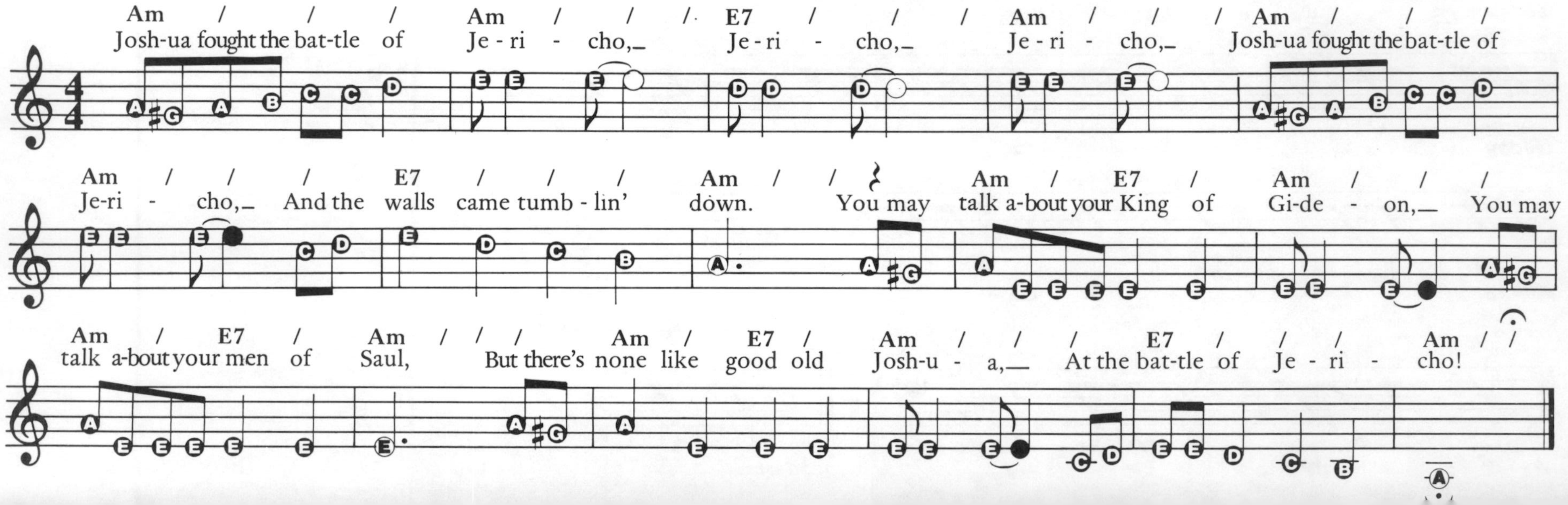

HOW TO PLAY THE E CHORD

Play slowly and evenly:

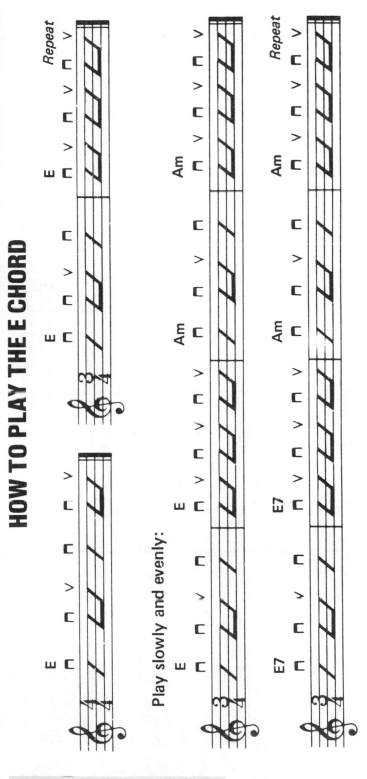

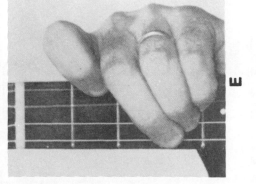

E

37

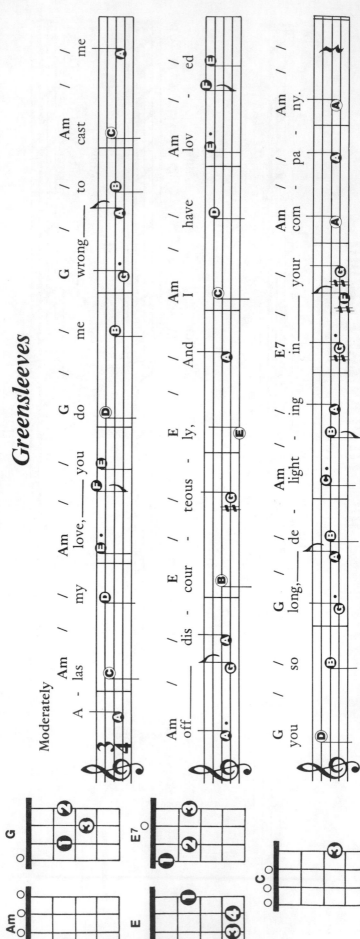

Greensleeves (cont.)

HOW TO PLAY THE C7 CHORD

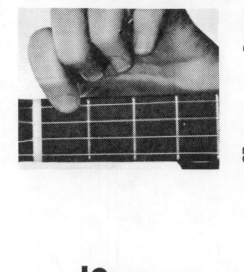

C7

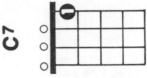

HOW TO PLAY THE F CHORD

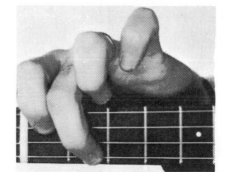

F

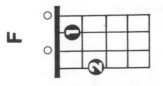

F AND C7 CHORDS
(cont.)

Play slowly and evenly:

I Know Where I'm Going

Moderately slow

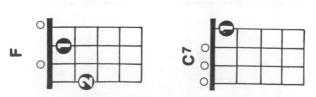

Oh, My Darling Clementine

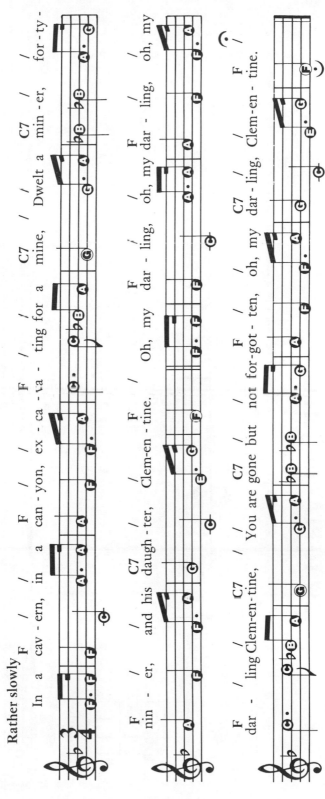

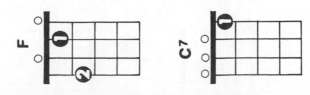

HOW TO PLAY IN $\frac{6}{8}$ TIME

Though $\frac{6}{8}$ time means there are 6 beats in each measure, it is usually accompanied as if it were $\frac{2}{4}$ time, or 2 beats per measure.

Vive L'Amour

Vive L'Amour (cont.)

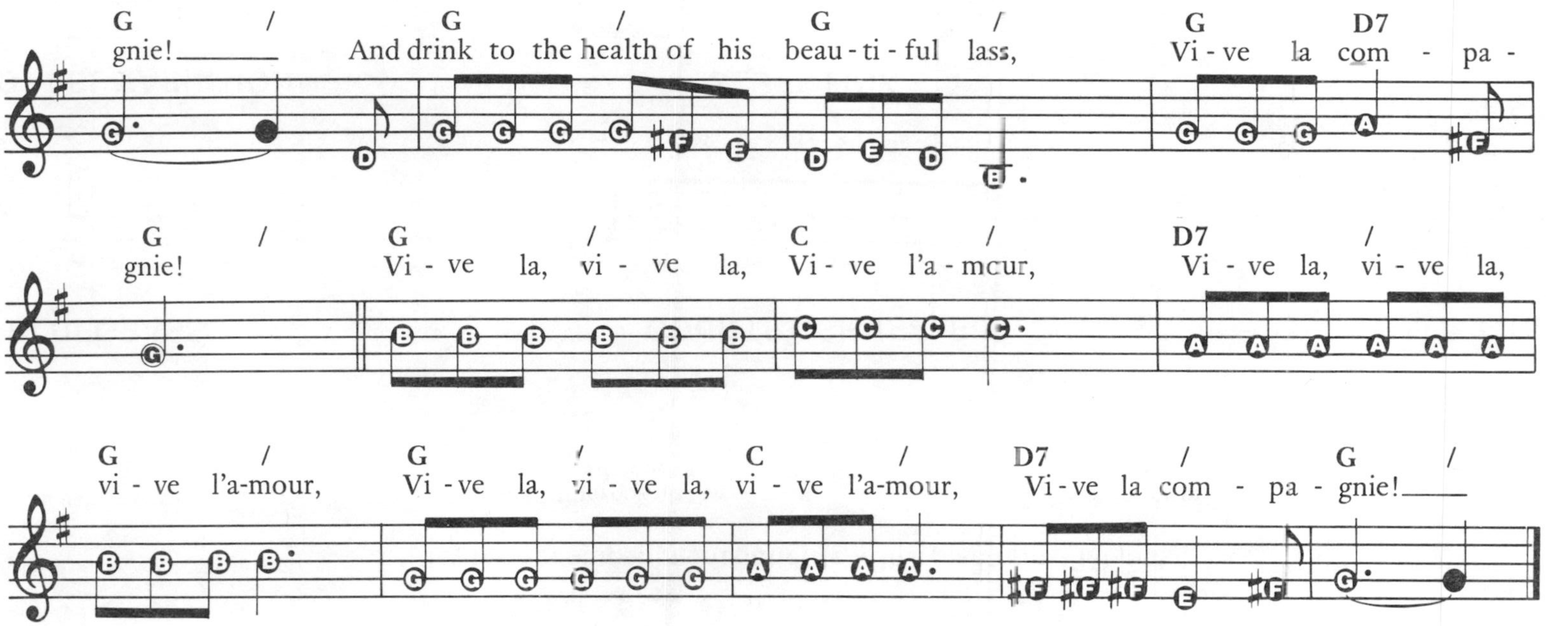

UKULELE ACCOMPANIMENTS

Play the accompaniment patterns with a plectrum (Flat-pick).

⊓ = strum down across the strings

∨ = strum up across the strings

/ = a slash means to strum the strings (use any chord)

> = accent or give emphasis

① = Circled numbers indicate the strings of the mandolin

②
③
④

BACK PICKING

Count: 1 & 2 & 3 & 4 &

GUITAR STRUM

Count: 1 2 3 4

COUNTRY-SHUFFLE

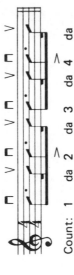

Count: 1 da 2 da 3 da 4 da

BLUES LICK

Count: 1 2 uh 3 4 uh

BLUEGRASS

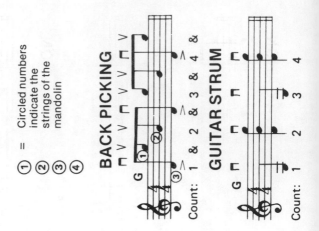

Count: 1 2 3 4

BLUEGRASS VARIATION

Count: 1 2 & 3 & 4 &

ACCOMPANIMENTS (cont.)

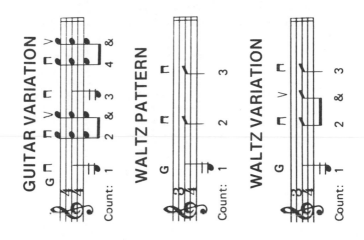

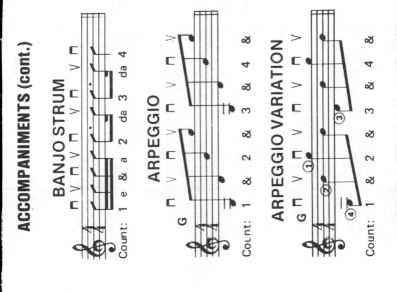

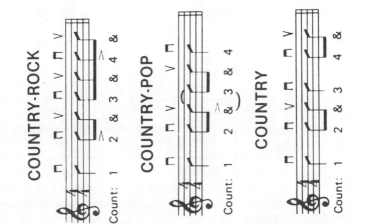

CHORD DERIVATIONS

Chords are derived from the notes of the major scale. The chart below indicates which notes of the scale make up each chord. A flat (♭) means to lower the scale note by one fret; a sharp (♯) means to raise the scale note by one fret.

CHORD	Notes of the Major Scale				
Major	1	3	5		
Minor	1	♭3	5		
7th	1	3	5	♭7	
9th	1	3	5	♭7	9
Augmented	1	3	♯5		
Diminished	1	♭3	♭5		
Major 6	1	3	5	6	
Minor 6	1	♭3	5	6	
Major 7	1	3	5	7	
Minor 7	1	♭3	5	♭7	
7th with Aug. 5	1	3	♯5	♭7	
7th with Dim. 5	1	3	♭5	♭7	

MAJOR KEYS AND RELATIVE MINORS

MAJOR KEY	RELATIVE MINOR KEY	KEY SIGNATURE
A♭	F	4♭
A	F♯	3♯
B♭	G	2♭
B	G♯	5♯
C♭	A♭	7♭
C	A	NO♯ NO♭
C♯	A♯	7♯
D♭	B♭	5♭
D	B	2♯
E♭	C	3♭
E	C♯	4♯
F	D	1♭
F♯	D♯	6♯
G♭	E♭	6♭
G	E	1♯

For a complete ukulele chord dictionary, see Alfred's Ukulele Chord Fingering Dictionary Handy Guide. It contains diagrams of all open string and moveable chords plus other helpful information.